Strange Weather Anthology

Strange Weather Anthology

True Quirks of Nature

Edited by
Marlene Mesot

Print layout, e-book conversion, and cover design by
DLD Books Editing and Self-Publishing Services
www.dldbooks.com

Cover photograph by Johannes Plenio

ISBN: 979-8-9858477-4-1

Contents

Introduction 7

With the Wind
    by Carol Farnsworth 9

A Bicycle Built for Two
    by Carol Farnsworth 13

Neptune's Revenge: Story of the Hurricane
    by Carol Farnsworth 15

Strange Rain Stories
    by Cleora Boyd 21

Spirit of the Rainbow
    by Cheryl McNeil Fisher 29

Harbor Squall
    by Ann Chiappetta 35

A Farmer's Prediction
    by Jackie Collins 39

A Giant's Snowballs
    by John Cronin 43

Balls of Fire
    by Leonard Tuchyner 47

Unusual Weather We're Having
    by Leonard Tuchyner 49

Tornado Outbreak
    by Lynda McKinney Lambert 53

Visibility
    by Lynda McKinney Lambert 59

Flashes in the Sky (Ballad Nonfiction)
        by Marlene Mesot...65

Split Screen Weather
        by Marlene Mesot...69

The Passion of Life's Storms
        by Patty L. Fletcher...77

Dodging Tornados in Tornado Alley
        by Robert D. Sollars..83

Introduction

These stories are true life adventures told by the people who experienced them. If you have only lived in one area of the world, the weather you experience may be quite different from the weather experienced in other parts. If you have moved around you will appreciate the distinct attitudes and preparations that are necessary to tackle different weather experiences.

I grew up in New Hampshire, so I am used to how New England handles snow. When my family moved to Virginia, for example, it seemed funny to us when the possibility of snow was announced, and then you went to the grocery store only to find the bread and milk shelves bare. We don't even start counting snow until it's at least a few inches to measure back home, but people seem to panic when the word is mentioned in southern Virginia. Before COVID school was canceled at the mention of freezing rain or snow. That is because some parts of our area are mountainous and students living in these areas would be at great risk trying to get to school under these conditions.

This leads me to discuss how this book came about. I was posting to my writers' group list when, on 31 January 2021, I mentioned the weather first. "Today we're having a mixed bag of weather. The snow is being friendly as it is staying off the hard surfaces, just covering the grass and trees and tops of cars etc. Then it rained and went to freezing rain. Now it's misting but the snow is holding for now."

Then, on 2 February 2021, in response to a six sentence writing challenge I wrote this:

Split Screen Weather Phenomenon
by Marlene Mesot
02/02/2021

There is a saying; if you don't like the weather wait a minute.

What about between the minutes?

Have you ever been in one place where the weather was, say sunny, but you could see beside you or ahead of you, a dark, windy, torrent of a rainstorm?

This has happened to me twice.

In fact, my website header is one of these pictures.

Mark my words, I'm not kidding.

From this post I received several responses from fellow writers remarking about their strange weather experiences. Then, in phone conversations, there were similar weather discussions. These occurrences prompted me to decide to gather these odd but true stories for a unique reading and visualizing experience. Thus, this anthology was born. It is my pleasure and privilege to bring these amazing accounts of true quirks of nature to a collection, all in one place, to be enjoyed and remembered.

Marlene Mesot

With the Wind

by Carol Farnsworth

On a sunny, sultry summer day,
My husband John, and I decided to ride a rails to trails.

The trailhead was the parking lot of an old abandon train
    station.

We unloaded the tandem, snapped on our helmets and headed
    North to Reed City.

The air was still and heavy with moisture.

I joked that we were creating our own rain as sweat trickled
    from under our helmets to drip down our faces and backs.

Setting a leisurely pace, we chatted about the growing crops,
    stopping to touch a wild flower, take a photo and buy ice
    cream.

When arriving in Reed City, the weather had taken a dramatic
    change.
The air felt cool and a breeze was blowing to the south.

Looking to the west, John saw a bank of heavy storm clouds
    blanketing the sky.
Quickly, we turned around as a clap of distant thunder was
    heard.
Normally, I am a slow biker.
I prefer to enjoy the ride and let my husband do most of the
    work.
But that day, I matched the speed and strength of John's
    peddling,
as we worked to stay ahead of the storm.
Our faces were hot and sweaty,
but the cold wind on our backs cooled us
while propelling us southward.
Our conversation was limited to a phrase that could be said in a
    quick breath.
"That thunder clap sounded closer."
"Pedal."
"Did you see that lightening strike?"
"Pedal!"
"I don't think we're going to make it!"
"PEDAL!"
Dodging a Jogger, we streaked into the Parking lot at full speed
    and in high gear.
Halting at the truck, I felt the first drops of rain hit my helmet.
Stowing the bike, we bolted for the cab, as a cascade of rain and
    the fireworks of the storm erupted all around us.

From *Leaf Memories* by Carol Farnsworth

Author Comments

Regarding my poem, "With the Wind", the first section has a blank line between each sentence to show a slow pace. The second section has no spaces. I found that the poem was spoken quicker by voice over screen reader this way.

A Bicycle Built for Two

by Carol Farnsworth

The best quote about tandeming was from another tandeming couple. No matter what direction your relationship is headed a tandem will get you there faster. My husband John and I have tandemed for over 21 years. We are more than recreational riders. Last year, we rode 1200 miles through the season. That is with me recovering from a broken pelvis. We average between two and three thousand miles a year.

We use the bike every day to go shopping and do other errands. Several times a week, we take longer rides on the many trails that surround us.

We have worn out three tandem bikes. Currently, we have a grey Trek tandem with a step through frame for me, while the captain has a normal raised bar. Collapsible baskets on both sides of the rear wheel are ready to be filled from our shopping.

I have found that experiencing nature while riding and the description of sights from John, keeps me a tuned to the natural wonders around me.

Neptune's Revenge:
Story of the Hurricane

by Carol Farnsworth

This occurred in the summer of 1972.
I was 17 and on a tour with a musical group of teens.

The crossing from Corfu to Tunisia would take one and a half days. At dinner that evening, the captain informed us that was a storm between us and the African coast. He advised us to eat light and use the belts provided on our bunks to prevent falling out of bed. I had wondered about the belt on my bunk. It was similar to a car's seat belt but longer. I laughed as I prepared for bed . I secured my belongings in the cabinet and belted myself to the bed.

Early in the morning I was awakened to the crashing of dishes and glasses breaking on the other side of the door to the kitchen. The small ship was rearing like a bronco. We crested a swell only to crash on the other side of the wave. Thanks to my buckling in, I stayed in my bed. My belongings weren't so lucky. I had bought a ceramic bottom drum for my younger brother. It crashed to the floor when the cabinet's door flew open. Later, I gathered up the pieces.

The ship completed turning into the wind and the floor was steady on my feet. My bunk mate was groaning softly. She jumped up and rushed to the bathroom. I followed her to assist. At the door to the bathroom, I was greeted with sounds of heaving and the smell of partly digested shrimp. I retreated to get dressed and get some fresh air on deck.

There were about ten of us that made it to the deck. We were the lucky ones. We weren't seasick and we were excited to watch the waves crash over the bow of the ship.

We edged closer to the bow to get a better view. A sailor looking a bit green, motioned us away and in broken English yelled, "Go down below!". We were reluctant to give up the fresh air but the wind and waves were getting worse.

We gathered in the lounge, located in midships and would have the least movement. Opening the game cabinet, we picked cards to play Uno. The cards slid across the table, as did our chairs. We moved to heavier pieces of furniture.

The morning progressed to noon. I was hungry. I asked if anyone had visited the dining room today?

No one had so myself and two other friends decided to make our way to get food for the group.

The cooks must have been as sick as the passengers. They put out two heavy bowls filled with oranges and yesterday's baked rolls. We gathered the food and avoiding the bathrooms, we headed back to the lounge.

By evening, we were able to return to our rooms and prepare for bed. The bathrooms had been cleaned and most of the passengers were not eating and staying in their bunks. I buckled in for another bumpy night.

Dawn broke over calm seas and the coast of Tunisia. At breakfast, most of us ate bread and tea or coffee. The captain informed us that the hurricane had blown us over 100 miles off course. We had landed in a small Muslim town not the large city of Tunis.

About Carol Farnsworth

Carol has worn many hats in her life. Musician, speech therapist, artist and poet. She has been published in many online magazines. In addition to publication in Magnets and Ladders, she has been published in the Avocet, Plum Tree Tavern, Spirit Fire Review and The Handy Uncapped Pen.

Born with glaucoma, Carol has experienced gradual vision loss all her life. Other passions are gardening, cooking and tandem biking. While riding as a stoker, she can discover nature through hearing, scent and touch. She and her tandem partner John live in a small town in western lower Michigan.

Publications

Leaf Memories, Carol Farnsworth, author/publisher, (1 August 2021).

Blog: Blind on the Lite Side: Traveling up and down the blind highway of life, Carol Farnsworth

John and Carol on Tandem on the White Pine Rail to Trail south of Reed City Michigan, 6/15/2020

John and Carol at Mount Rogers State Park

Strange Rain Stories

by Cleora Boyd

Creeped Out

I bagged the trash and headed out the door. All the slots under the car port of the two story apartment building across from the apartment I was living in during the mid-1980s, were filled. One resident was turning down the North side of their building. Probably Headed for the laundry room. It was too early for the office to be open, and most people were still asleep at this hour on a Saturday morning.

Following the landing, I skipped down the stairs and turned toward the dumpsters at the South end of the complex. It was a bright sunny spring morning. But, Around the fourth or fifth car on my side, I slowed. I had a disturbing feeling I was being followed. I looked behind me. The light was dim in the early morning dawn. There was no one there. Ahead of me, the sun was shining brightly. Hmm, I thought and walked on, but I couldn't shake the feeling. I checked behind me again. There was a slight breeze, and the air felt heavy and damp. Suddenly, I realized it was darker behind me than in front. I looked up. Spread over the access road between the two buildings, and just high enough to pass over was a dark grey cloud creeping along at the speed I was walking. I stopped and stared at it. It seemed to stop. It wasn't raining. Everything in front and behind me was dry. I looked up again. I definitely had a dark low hanging cloud on my tail. I decided to go ahead and take the trash to the dumpster as planned and quickened my pace. I glanced up from time to time. It was still there, keeping pace with me. At the dumpster, I tossed in the bag, and was then gripped with the realization I was going to have to somehow get around this ominous cloud and back to my apartment.

By now, the edge of the cloud was just above me. The carport for my building was a few feet away. Rain began to fall as I arrived under the cover of the first spot. I walked along under the port until I reached the slot next to the stairs up to my apartment. I watched the cloud migrate lazily along until I could go up the stairs without getting wet. Grinning and shaking my head, I wondered how I could have been so creeped out by a big, dark, low hanging, slow-moving cloud, and hurried to my computer to record the experience.

Discriminating Rain

Ten or fifteen years later, I had moved into a house. It was an early summer day, and I had come home for lunch. I hit the garage door opener button and drove into my garage.

In the kitchen, I went about the business of making my lunch. Then I noticed water running off my house. But, I thought, it's not raining. My first assumption was that some kids were playing a practical joke by using a hose to run water on my roof. I went to the patio window. Sheets of water were pouring off the roof and I could see drops from a heavy rain beating down on the patio. Perplexed, I went to the front door. The sun was shining brightly, and there was not a drop of water to be seen. At the patio window, a heavy rain continued to fall. Okay, I thought. What are the chances? The rain lasted for several minutes and only fell in the back yard. Not a single drop fell in the front.

Angry Rain

On May 11, 1970, I was watching the Carol Burnett Show. They were singing "Raindrops Are Falling On My Head." Outside, raindrops were falling, and the program was being frequently interrupted with reports of potentially dangerous storms in the area of Wolfforth--a town several miles to the Northwest of our location. My roommate and I were living in an apartment building with eight three room apartments. Four on the first floor and 4 on the second. Our apartment was on the first floor across from the manager. Our door was open. The heat that day had been oppressive. Driving home from school, it felt like the heat was bouncing off the asphalt. I had planned to visit my friend at Lubbock Christian College, but because the heat was so oppressive, I told Barbara, "Let's go home, We can visit her in the morning before she leaves." Having grown up in the panhandle of Texas, I was quite used to thunderstorms. I kept telling my friend there was nothing to worry about. I didn't know why people always got so excited about a heavy rain. I remembered my folks standing at the back porch window when we had a storm. I realize now, they were watching the clouds for tornadic activity. When they were young, the technology we have today didn't exist, and people knew how to "read the clouds" so they could take shelter if necessary. At that time, I had never seen or been in a tornado. Strangely enough, while I was assuring Barbara there was nothing to worry about, I was going around the apartment storing everything I could either in the closet or in a drawer. Barbara watched me, mystified.

Suddenly, the manager came to our door. "Come on," he ordered. "We have to get into the basement."

Everyone in the building was rounded up and we were ushered down the stairs into the cellar. As soon as the musty smell of dirt reached my nostrils, I wanted to turn around and run back out, but my way was blocked by the other residents. As the tornado passed over, I felt dirt falling on my head. It sounded like the building was being lifted up. Eventually everything settled down as the danger passed. As it happens, we were at the outer edge of the storm.

We came out and surveyed the damage. The man in the apartment on the top Southeast corner had moved his truck up beside the building to protect it. This was the only corner of the building that was damaged, and the wind had dropped the debris on his vehicle after depositing a tree trunk in their tub. For this reason, I refuse to take shelter in a tub during a storm. This man, we learned from his wife, had left to go looting as soon as we came out of the basement. In our apartment, the glass in the windows in our living room was blown completely out, but, the curtains were hanging as if nothing had happened. My research paper that was due on Monday, was soaked. Not sure why it hadn't been one of the things I put in a drawer. The red pot with my Jacobs plant was still sitting on the window sill, well-watered, and undisturbed. None of the leaves were so much as nicked, and There weren't any pieces of glass or debris in the pot. The apartment building to the north looked like a building under construction. The roof was gone, there was no glass in any of the windows, and no furniture was visible in any of the rooms. To the north of that building, the house had collapsed into the basement killing all inside. In contrast to the earlier intense heat, it was uncomfortably cold, and a heavy fish smell hung in the air.

A brick had crashed through the back window of Barbara's car. The glass was completely gone, but nothing else was damaged. There was no piece of glass or brick that was larger than the tip of my little finger.

The Citizen Bank Tower was visibly twisted. I don't know to what angle, but it was like a giant hand had reached down and turned it clockwise. If you stood at a distance, you could watch it sway back and forth. The news speculated that there may have been as many as 300 tornadoes in the area that night.

For years. When a storm came up I would go to a friend's house that had a bomb shelter until the storm passed. I stopped doing that after one night when I was on my way, I had to drive through flooded streets. Water seeped into my car and soaked my feet in the floorboard of the car. As I was driving down 19th Street, I heard a roar over my head that might have been a tornado passing over. The next day, the news reported that there had been a movement in the cloud at about where I was at that time. After that, I decided I was safer staying where ever I was. Now, that I no longer drive, I have no other choice. After I moved to Fort Worth, I would relive that experience every time I drove under a railroad track with a train passing overhead. It sounds much the same as what I heard in the basement that night. The PTSD from this experience lasted close to 50 years. I didn't even realize that was what it was until all the discussion of soldier's returning from war torn areas. I can definitely understand the affect a terrifying experience can have on one's life.

Slanted Rain

When I was young, we lived on a little acreage out in the country off Highway 214. One evening in the late '50s or early '60s, I was standing on the front porch looking to the east. There, one or so miles away, was a small dark cloud with what looked like dark yarn streaming down to the ground at roughly a five degree angle. It took a while for me to realize I was watching it rain in the distance. The cloud was either moving very slowly, or there was a light breeze blowing under the cloud just enough to cause the rain to fall at an angle.

Pulling Trees

One evening in 2000, a thunder storm came through my neighborhood. That is not unusual in an area referred to as tornado alley. Having been in a tornado, I was nervous. I opened my front door to look out. The Arizona Elm with a 45 foot canopy was twisting and bunched together at the top like a huge hand had grasped it and was trying to pull it up.

It is easy to think that whatever is happening weatherwise where we are is also happening everywhere else around us, but that is not the case. I'm not sure I would have realized that if it hadn't been for the experience of the cloud between the apartment buildings or the one over my house. In Fort Worth, it is not unusual to drive through torrential rain for a mile or two and then ride for a while in bright sunshine where it is totally dry before driving through another distance of heavy rain. In the case of the cloud over my house, maybe it started to drop its rain as it moved past the middle of my roof, and then continued south, never dropping any rain on the front; similar to the cloud that was moving between the apartment buildings. What is interesting to me, is that all of these clouds, if moving, were either moving North or South, not East or West.

About Cleora Boyd

As a person with Retinitis Pigmentosa, Cleora Boyd first pursued a career in Accounting. After receiving a Bachelor of Science degree in Math from Texas Tech University in Lubbock, Texas, she went on to obtain employment with a major pharmaceutical corporation in Fort Worth, Texas, where she still lives.

After careers in accounting and computer science, Cleora Boyd turned to creative writing to express herself during her retirement. Some of her creations can be found in the periodicals *Magnets & Ladders*, *Consumer Vision*, and *Slate and Style*.

She also writes under the pen names C. S. Boyd and Sly Duck. Living in Fort Worth, Texas, Cleora enjoys reading, writing, and watching TV with her Cockatiel, Dusty.

Spirit of the Rainbow

by Cheryl McNeil Fisher

Have you ever seen a rainbow? Most of the time, they are faint shades of color arching through the sky. The colors in a rainbow are red, orange, yellow, green, blue, indigo and violet. The fascination begins as a child. An adult in our life yells excitedly, "Look at the rainbow. Can you see all the colors?" I never could make out all seven colors unless seeing it in a book or coloring one myself. And let's not forget that pot of gold waiting at the end. My little brain used to wonder how to get there, not knowing that the gold has always been within my reach.

...that had in it all the colors of the rainbow. This was the dazzling light that shows the presence of the Lord.
Ezekiel 12:28 Good News Bible.

One late afternoon, I was driving west across the Newburgh/Beacon Bridge in the Mid–Hudson Valley of New York. Out of the corner of my eye, I saw a bright orange color and glanced in my rear–view mirror. I was absolutely dazzled by a brilliant rainbow. I exited immediately after the toll and parked in a lot. I stood outside of my car and looked in wonder. I thought, "Wow, God! Wow!" I don't know how long I stood there with a smile on my face. My prayers were of thanksgiving that God loved me so much that he painted the sky just for me!

Two months later, I was driving my car and saw a flash of light. I knew what had happened because I experienced retinal detachments the year before, resulting in the loss of my sight in my right eye.

Fortunately, I was less than a mile from my house. The following day I was back in New York City for surgery, beginning a new journey in my life. I never once said, "God, why did this happen? Why did you do this to me." The snow crunched under my feet as I left my home. I stopped, inhaled the crisp cool air, and looked up to a clear blue sky. I took in every bare branch and prayed, "God help me. I may never see a tree again." And guess what God did; he put the idea of a guide dog in my spirit.

My surgeon insisted that I would never need a guide dog. Well, a renowned eye doctor told my mother that when others begin to lose their sight after forty, mine would get better.

t'I didn know anyone with a guide dog or anything about them. And why did I suddenly know that one day I would? I believe God gave me the calming knowledge to give me hope during the multiple surgeries and loss to come.

When the rainbow appears in the clouds, I will see it and remember the everlasting covenant between me and all living beings on earth.
Genesis 9:16.

I may not see rainbows with my eyes, but I continue to see them and feel them in my spirit. A rainbow is God's promise and love. There have been many dark times, but I have always known, God is with me, and I can begin my day over as many times as I need; even just before I fall asleep, I say, "Thank you, God, for loving me and for helping me be the best that I can be."

About Cheryl McNeil Fisher

Cheryl McNeil Fisher is someone who knows about life s challenges. In study after study, it has been shown that adjusting to blindness is the most difficult experience we as humans can go through. But beyond just getting by, in Cheryl we find someone who had good vision and a lucrative career, having to tap into inner and spiritual resources to not be stopped when others well might give up. She has earned a four year degree in counseling from the State University of New York as well as the divinity program of Bethel University. A resident of the Hudson Valley area of New York, Cheryl has expanded her scope of motivational and educational initiatives beyond the northeast to a nation–wide outreach. You can find her speaking about finding the strength to face setbacks and then excel plus she is an advocate for children and adults with a full spectrum of differently special traits.

But her vision expands to include writing and publishing her own books, for children but with a message for adults there too. Cheryl is the author of Cindy Lou and Sammy Too Go to the Mall, The Adventure of a Guide Dog Team(2014) and the SPECIAL EDITION with Discussion Questions (2016), Apple Batter–Up (2015), Lightning in NABBED (2016) and the owner of Doggoneit Publishing, a private book label dedicated to producing quality books.

She also focuses on literacy and writing, sharing her love of reading and encouraging students to develop the same love. In addition, Cheryl offers workshops for children about how to develop a story, write a book, and illustrate a book. In her storybook workshop students produce a 12–page book with personalized front and back covers. She hopes to engender the love of reading and writing in children and to foster creativity while learning about special needs individuals at the same time.

Website: www.cherylmcneilfisher.com

Publications

Fiction

The Adventure of a Guide Dog Team Series:
1 *Cindy Lou and Sammy Too Go to the Mall*, by Cheryl McNeil Fisher, Doggoneit Publishing, (2014).
Cindy Lou and Sammy Too Go to the Mall, Cheryl McNeil Fishe, Audio by Chris Abernathy (19 August 2016).
2 *Cindy Lou and Sammy Too Meet New Friends at the Zoo*, Cheryl McNeil Fisher, Doggoneit Publishing (16 August 2016).
Cindy and Sammy Meet New Friends at the Zoo, Cheryl McNeil Fisher, Audio by Chris Abernathy (14 December 2022).
3 *Surprise Sammy! It's Your Birthday*, Cheryl McNeil Fisher, Illustrator Anastasia Moshkarina, Doggoneit Publishing (1 February 2017).
4 *History Mystery in Philadelphia*, Cheryl McNeil Fisher, author/publisher, Illustrator Anastasia Moshkarina, (30 September 2022).

Sister Shenanigans' Series:
Apple Batter–Up, Cheryl McNeil Fisher, Doggoneit Publishing (2016, 13 April 2022).
Hootin Holliday, Cheryl McNeil Fisher, Doggoneit Publishing (2016, 21 October 2022).

Bolter & Lightning in NABBED, Cheryl McNeil Fisher, Anastasia Moshkarina (Illustrator), Doggoneit Publishing (22 February 2016).
NABBED, Cheryl McNeil Fisher, Audio by Chris Abernathy, (3 March 2017).

Nonfiction

Time Capsule: A Memoir Denice Maier Reale Saunders, by Cheryl McNeil Fisher, author/publisher, 21 May 2022).

Visionary Series Co-Authored:
1 *Writing Works Wonders Creative Writing Prompt Journal*, Cheryl McNeil Fisher and Dr. Kathleen P. King, et al. Writing Works Wonders, (18 April 2022).
2 *Writing Works Wonders Web Design for Authors*, Cheryl McNeil Fisher and Dr. Kathleen P. King, et al. Writing Works Wonders, (15 April 2023).

Harbor Squall

By Ann Chiappetta

The unmistakable sulfurous stink of low tide thick with humidity and sea smells brings me back to the fondest recollections of childhood. I developed from a motion sick land lubber into a confident first mate, thanks to a divorce, cabin cruiser named Sea Luv and the wiles of Mother Nature.

New York is brutal in the summer. We got a reprieve from the heat and humidity on the boat, trolling offshore for hours, pulling in blues and hoping for stripers....It would get roasting and Dad would slide the boat into neutral and we'd plunge into the cool depths, pop out, and climb back aboard. We would never admit the brevity of the quick dip was due to the fear of sharks.

Dad taught me the best way to finesse a fiddler crab onto a hook, mix chum, and remove hooks and so much more. We didn't water-ski often, it wasted gas for fishing

One of my most defining moments played out during an attempt to outrun a squall. It bore down on us in minutes. We were heading back from a quick run. There were six of us, Dad, me, my stepmother and her sister-in-law and her two kids. Dad watched the black clouds, rising winds and white caps and his face grew serious. He made everyone secure their lifejackets and sent them all into the cabin.

"Stay calm and don't come up on deck unless I tell you," he said to them.

I got different instructions.

"None of them can help, they're all panicking. It's me and you. Hold on and do what I say,"

He motioned to the wheel,

"Don't let go,"

His arms tightened with effort, wrestling with the wheel,...forcing the boat to head for the little island, stern to the screaming wind. I understood it meant saving us from capsizing. Landing on the beach was better than sinking.

Before Dad lost control, he grabbed me, looked into my face, and said,

"If I get hurt, you make sure you send the mayday,"

I gave him a stiff nod, braced myself against the console and held the shuddering, uncooperative wheel. Dad worked the throttle and we both hung on. The waves pelted us, the deck pitched me like a doll, slamming me into the dash. The sound was deafening. It was as if a watery hand grabbed and slammed us onto the beach, then it was over, we were taking on water, and my ears were ringing.

"Go check on them," said Dad, "

I opened the door and met four pairs of frightened eyes.

"We're up on the beach, , it's over,"

I heard Dad sending the mayday and the tension in my shoulders eased. In less than an hour we were towed off the shore, bailed out most of the water, fired up the engine, and chugged back to the dock.

Later, after a well-deserved clam strip dinner at IHOP, Dad said,

"Could've been worse,"

Our eyes met,

"I thought you were going to be scared but you weren't," he said, a pleased expression on his tanned face.

"Thanks, Dad," I said.

He resumed dipping his clam strips into the tartar sauce and seemed to enjoy each bite.

About Ann Chiappetta

Ann Chiappetta author and multi-media specialist.
Making meaningful connections.

The author of five fiction and nonfiction books, Ann's poems, creative nonfiction, essays and fiction appear in anthologies, online magazines, blogs and small press reviews.

Annie is also co-host of the Art Parlor Podcast produced by Friends in Art of the American Council of the Blind and she visits schools and organizations in Westchester County presenting a disability awareness and people with disabilities program to K-6 grade students.

All things Annie: www.annchiappetta.com

Anne Chiappetta

A Farmer's Prediction

by Jackie Collins

My father stopped shoveling the dirt near the irrigation ditch to gaze at the sky. "Smells like a storm's coming." He and Grandpa could predict the elements, could smell hail long before seeing it, like a fox smells naïve chickens bedded down for the night outside the chicken coop. It was mid–July in Nebraska and the air was close and heavy enough to have a distinct presence, to invade the nostrils the perfect combination for a storm. We shoveled fast, sweating harder as perspiration soaked our bodies, aware the yet unseen was stirring in the west. We needed to finish digging that afternoon because hopefully for us, the storm would arrive during early evening instead.

An hour later, my father leaned on his shovel handle, a support and relief for his painful back. He raised his head up to assess dark clouds inching toward us, their form like upside down hamburger buns squeezed together. Thus, my twelve year–old and oldest sister, Vicki, named them "puffy buns", a perfect description. "Looks like someone's gonna' get hailed on today. Look how dark those clouds are, green too."

Following his gaze, I looked as heavy greenish-gray rolling clouds morphed from puffy buns into gigantic bowling balls across our distant pasture. The static in the air bristled my skin, nature's warning before danger strikes.

The storms always approached from the same direction, rising over the hilly land ten miles to the west until they formed an immense bank, as we called it, a forceful body enveloping the sky, drawing near. Still, I loved the excitement, how we ran like crazy to the tractor, our shovels in hand and hopped on, racing the sky to the house's safety before sizzling bolts of lightning arrived. More than once, a farmer had been killed on his tractor, staying out too long in the field, ignoring the flashes of danger.

We scurried into our porch, my heart pounded as we watched through the windows. Wind forced solid oak tree branches to acquiesce into a sharp angle, some cracking as they gave in. Thunder rumbled, its deep voice carrying over our yard. Clouds twisted all directions in the sky, the familiar sign of a tornado. We held our breath, waiting for a tail to drop and spin through our yard to whip everything into debris, whirling them around and slamming all to the ground. Possibly, our house.

"See, there's a tail coming down!" My father said as a dark extension swung from a nearing cloud in the west.

My mother quickly said, "You kids get in the basement."

We were so accustomed to such storms and disappointed, hoped we could stay on the porch. I found the danger enticing and ignored possibility of harm, a trait ingrained from my father. Ignore safety. There's work to be done. This time, he ignored his own rule.

We knew better than to disobey. Charging down the steps, we hurried to peer out of small windows located at the top of the cement walls. My sisters, brother and I rushed back and forth between them, only able to see the front yard's grass lean over and a multitude of leaves flying over it. I went back to the steps and gazed up to see my mother's backside as she paced from window to window. My father stayed in one spot, silent as he stared at our cornfield to the east, worried hail would drop. If hail battered our crops, our year's living income would be wiped out, forcing us to borrow money at the discretion of the local town's bank, making him beholden and ashamed.

Finally, our parents let us up from the basement. The tornado had swept over our farmyard without dropping its tail. No destroyed buildings, but still a mess left in its wake. The fierce gale lifted the ungrounded debris, tossing it around the yard. Loosened tree branches, rolls of unbound wire, broken fence boards, green leaves and more spread over the yard, a blanket of trash.

Soon the storm passed, and though we had a few sprinkles of rain, our crops stood tall and erect. "Bet someone got hailed," my father replied. Vicki pointed to the blanket of clouds moving away from us and to the east. "There go the puffy buns!" She was right. This time, someone's crops had been hailed. We were lucky this time.

We stepped outside into the cool air as my father headed to the garage to get the pick–up.

"Let's go for a ride. See if anyone had damage." It's what farmers did after a storm. Survey damage. Either their own or someone else's. We kids hopped onto the pick–up bed, riding on the tailgate, our dog Trixie between us, slobbering on our bare legs shivering from the cool metal beneath.

My mother and father sat in the front and we drove slowly as we pursued the trail of the storm, seeing who got rain or hail, who didn't, and assessing the damage of fields. More than one farm had been hailed upon, the farms not far from us. It had stripped stalks of corn, smashing them into the ground, stealing the stalk's life with its ears of corn a family's living. We felt bad for those fields damaged, yet relieved ours had been missed. Pure luck. Such was the nature of farming, a never–ending gamble. That day, we won.

About Jackie Collins

Jackie Collins lives in Berthoud, Colorado, in the front range of the Rocky Mountains. A retired speech therapist, she loves spending as much time as possible in their rugged beauty. She is passionate about animals, especially dogs and along with her husband of fifty years, lives with their canine child Rusty. Raised on a farm in central Nebraska, she has written an unpublished memoir about the valuable, and also volatile disappearing culture and lifestyle. She and her husband have three children and four grandchildren, which she claims she can never see enough. Writing solo for many years at home, during lunch breaks and recesses at school, along with her writing group of twenty–five years, has been her compass in life.

Publications

Telling Tales and Sharing Secrets by Jackie Collins, Diana Kinared and Sally Showalter, Atmosphere Press, 6 September 2022

Blog: A Way with Words by Jackie Collins, Diana Kinared and Sally Showalter

Jackie Collins

A Giant's Snowballs

by John Cronin

Jumping from the bed into the wheelchair, I quickly rolled into the kitchen for breakfast.

Before I could say anything, mom pointed out the west window exclaiming, "Look outside! Have you ever seen anything like that before? The whole field is covered with them. Some must be three feet high."

Turning the wheelchair for a better view, I beheld the most amazing sight I had ever seen in my seventeen years. Wherever I looked the field was covered by snowballs. There were big ones, small ones, and in between sizes.

Turning to mom, I blurted out, "Wow! It looks like giants were rolling snowballs all night. Have you ever seen anything like this before?"

"Never," was mom's reply. "I wonder if the wind I heard last night had anything to do with it."

"I have no idea," I replied, "but I can hardly wait to get out there and check them out. I wonder if they are hard like a snowball that turns into an ice ball. Thanks Mom," I said when she placed a bowl of hot oatmeal before me.

"Take your time!" Mom ordered. "Don't eat like a pig. The snow is not going to evaporate before you get outside."

Mumbling through a mouthful of porridge I replied, "Maybe not, but I can hardly wait to find out about them. I think they are going to be fun to play with."

With hot food in my stomach and teeth brushed I wheeled to the laundry room where my snowmobile suit hung. Pulling on the suit, boots, mitts, scarf, and helmet, the last items I grabbed were my crutches. Standing with the crutches and leg braces, I felt like a knight of old, ready to joust with the giant makers of the snowballs.

Outside I pulled the cover from my mighty steed, making sure it was well fed with gas and oil. Strapping the crutches to the snowmobile's running boards like a pair of saddlebags, I mounted my yellow steed. After a couple of yanks on the pull cord, my mount barked to life. With my thumb jammed hard on the throttle I was soon roaring across the yard, making a beeline for the nearest large snowball. Not knowing how the snowball was constituted, I took my time when approaching the giant's ball. It was the height of the snowmobile windshield. Reaching out with my mitten hand I slapped the snowball, but not hard enough to hurt my hand if the ball was hard. I was instantly enveloped in a cloud of fluffy cold snow, as the ball exploded.

While the snowmobile idled beneath me, I whispered to myself, "Wow! Bursting these snowballs is going to be one heck of a lot of fun. I smash into them and get showered with snow. First, I had better make sure that all the snowballs are fluffy. I do not want to slam into an ice ball. That would bring my snowmobiling career to a rapid end."

Driving to another ball, I poked it with a ski. Poof! Another one burst. This time I spurred my steed into a gallop, pointed it at the chosen victim and charged. Like before, the ball burst, however this time I was completely enveloped in a cloud of cold soft snow.

"This is great!" I yelled to the sky. "How many can I smash?"

Charging around the field, I smashed every one of the giant's snowballs I could find. It did not take long before a friend joined me. He'd seen the snowballs and could not resist investigating. Soon Jim and I commenced smashing balls left and right. We competed trying to see who could demolish the most snowballs. We played a game of "Top Gun," trying to get the highest score. Before long, we cleared all the balls from half the field. At this point, we drew our machines together for a chat.

I asked, "Hey Jim have you ever seen anything like this before?"

"No." Jim replied. "Are these snowballs spread over all the fields? We almost destroyed all the ones in this field. We must find more. Let's go by Larry's farm and see if there are any there."

With the decision made, we both roared off. We were not disappointed. Wherever we looked, we could see the giant's handiwork. Immediately we set to work bursting balls. As the day wore on and dusk descended, Jim and I headed to our respective homes. Our steeds needed some rest after a day's jousting with a giant's handiwork.

I learned later that what occurred was very rare. Mom was correct when she asked if the wind was partly the cause. Because we were in the midst of a February thaw, the snow was the correct texture for the wind to blow the snow into snowballs. The different sized snowballs were the result of how long the wind had been able to push the ball over the sticky snow. Stronger winds or different surfaces resulted in different sized snowballs. Whatever the reason it took herculean strength to make a giant's snowball.

About John Cronin

The sixty–six–year–old John spends most of his time reading, writing and visiting with friends. He has one sister and six step siblings. In his childhood he contracted polio, leaving him a paraplegic.

Later he attended the University of Waterloo where he obtained a Bachelor of Arts degree in philosophy and political science, and a Master of Arts degree in philosophy. While working on his Ph. D. John's vision finally deteriorated to where he was legally blind due to Retinitis Pigmentosa.

Unable to continue his studies John decided to travel. He resided in Texas with a close friend from university. Later he traveled to Jamaica where he lived off and on for a few years. While in Jamaica he met and married Gillian White. They now reside on an acre in rural Ontario, near Cargill, not far from Lake Huron.

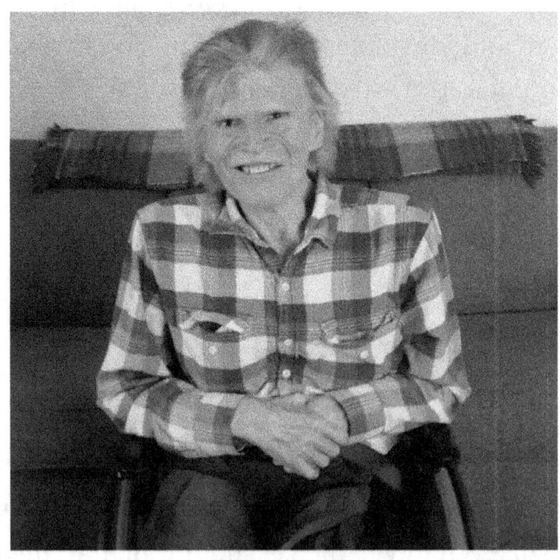

John Cronin

Balls of Fire

by Leonard Tuchyner

It was 1980 in Central Virginia, and I was on my way home. That is a simple sentence. We don't usually think of going home from work as a difficult or momentous task. But it was. Let me explain. I lived about 20 miles from my house in Ruckersville. My means of transportation was a bicycle. I needed to use a bike, because of my sight. You see, I can't see all that well. I'm legally blind. But I could see well enough for the slow speed of a bicycle. As I said, I was on my way home.

My route was completely on secondary roads that ran past farms, widely scattered houses and other countrified objects, as is befitting a rural area. The weather was threatening. Very threatening. The sky was dark. It was already evening, but this was almost as dark as night, and an ominous atmosphere pervaded. I expected it to storm before I reached home.

Sure enough, the droplets came. There is a section of the road on Route 20 which is full of twists and turns. Then the road straightens, and one has a clear view of the fields surrounding the road on both sides. Before I was out of the twisty place, it really started coming down. By the time I reached the open area, the lightning and thunder started. The thunder was so loud it shook my bones. I was really frightened of being hit. I was afraid of the bolts striking nearby and sending a current up past the tires and sending it into my body. I don't know whether that is realistic, but I was afraid to get off the bike. As far as I knew, the narrow rubber wheels were some protection.

As I came out of the last bend and viewed the fields in front and on either side of me, I saw something out of Hell. The lightning was taking the form of balls that flew across the fields. They were red, to my memory. But they could have been blue, as well.

I was in the middle of a war between Heaven and Hell. There was no place to hide. I didn't dare get off the bike, for reasons already described. As I said, there was no place to go even if I could get down. 'Keep going' was the word of the day. I was as wet as I had ever been coming out of the ocean. I was completely vulnerable. At least, it felt like that. Did I mention, I was not wearing a shirt? The reason I didn't wear a shirt was because of the weather. This was Central Virginia in the summer. You get sweaty really fast. So, I kept going...until the storm passed.

I have never witnessed ball lightening before and don't know of anyone who has. I have heard of it. It is really something you don't want to experience when riding a bike without even a shirt for protection. I know I don't want to ever again.

Unusual Weather We're Having

by Leonard Tuchyner

"Hey Una, what's that up ahead?" I asked, my throat tightening up suddenly.

"I don't know. Maybe you'd better slow down."

I might have done that, but it was suddenly upon us. The anomaly was a darkened area of the road immediately ahead of us. Our speed suddenly slowed to 20 from a rate of 60 mph.

The Volkswagen began to shake as we entered what later turned out to be a mini tornado. I thought that I'd better get through the thing as quickly as I could, if I could stay on the road. If the wind had not hit us directly on from the front, or if it had come at us from the side, we'd have been in either the Everglades or the canal running along to our left.

This was in the mid–sixties on Route 40 on our way home to Miami from St. Petersburg. Anyone knows, who has driven a Volkswagen of that vintage, that they were sadly underpowered with little to no aerodynamic properties. I drove a low–powered box smack into a tornado. My three kids and a cat were in the back and my wife, at the time, was Una Marie. None of them were saying anything. I think they were holding their breaths.

Thank God it was only a very small tornado. It took only minutes to drive through. I'd down shifted to second gear. As we left the twister, now without resistance, the bus began to pick up speed, and soon we were racing down the highway in fourth gear.

"Wow! That was something." I was seeing in the rear–view mirror what the others were looking at directly through the rear window. We could see the definite shape of a funnel. It was following us.

"Can you outrun it?" one of the kids asked.

I was leaving it behind rather quickly. "Yeah, but keep your eye on it. It could pick up speed."

It followed us for about four miles before veering off the highway. We could see it disappearing in the background behind us. We never saw it again. I never ran into one of those afterward, and for that I'm grateful.

I have lost a great deal of my sight since then.

That was not the only time I encountered strange weather phenomena in Florida, or with twisters. In this next episode I was not personally involved. Two people I worked with were. This was two years after I had received my degree in Rehabilitation Counseling at the University of Florida and was working for the state in that capacity.

Two people, David and Bill, who were also employed as counselors, had just purchased a yacht which was harbored at a Miami marina. This was a major purchase for them, and they had hardly had time to enjoy it when they received news from the harbor master that they'd better get down to the marina and see what had happened to their boat.

When they got there, they were sad to see remnants of their new purchase upside down in its mooring place in the docking area. It was the only boat that had been damaged by a small tornado that had touched down to lift their boat, turn it topsy turvy, and drop it in its own rightful anchorage.

Who knew that nature was so conniving as to precisely do damage to one boat? These men must have felt that they had a bull's–eye painted on their backs. Neptune must have had it in for them.

About Leonard Tuchyner

Leonard has had Stargardt's disease, which was first noticed in his teenaged years. He is now eighty–two. He reads through the media of braille, recordings, and electronic voices produced by Open Book and Zoom Text. He lives with his wife of forty-three years and their two dogs.

He is active in the local writing community, which includes attending critique groups. He also facilitates a Writing for Healing and Growth group at the Charlottesville Senior Center and facilitates three critique groups for Behind Our Eyes Writers with Disabilities group.

He has published *A Journey to Elsewhere – Poetry Through the Seasons of Life*, Cedar Creek Publishing, (22 March 2014) and been featured in several Skyline Anthology editions from Central Virginia Writers.

His hobbies include Tai Chi and gardening.

Website: https://www.dldbooks.com/tuchyner/

Publications

A Journey to Elsewhere – Poetry Through the Seasons of Life, by Leonard Tuchyner, Cedar Creek Publishing, (22 March 2014).

Merlyn the Magic Turtle: A Story of Love and Justice, by Leonard Tuchyner, author/publisher, (22 May 2022).

Tornado Outbreak

by Lynda McKinney Lambert

Thirty–six years ago, my dear friend, Rosella, had a brilliant idea in late March. So, naturally, she was anxious to share it with me. With her newest copy of our favorite artist magazine in her hand, she quickly turned to the page she had marked near the back of the magazine. "Here it is!" she announced as she pointed to a small advertisement.

"Lynda, I think we could do this! There will be an outdoor painting workshop in the Pocono Mountains! Look at the advertisement. We could even earn college credit by taking this course. Wouldn't it be fun to paint every day in the mountains with other artists?"

We called the phone number listed in the advertisement and requested more information. We filled out the necessary forms when the materials arrived. The 10–day workshop was a unique program in Plein air landscape painting created by two art professors. One taught at Rutgers University, and the other taught at Philadelphia School of Art.

Rosella's idea seemed innocent enough at the time. However, I now recognize that this decision was a pivotal moment that would take me in a new direction. There was a quiet tornado brewing inside of me because this course would be my first step in the academic environment of the art world. I wanted to go. Nevertheless, I felt afraid. It was a feeling that I was heading into dangerous unknown territory. In fact, I was.

By the spring of 1985, I had painted just about every day for nine years. I was reading about art, art history, and artists exclusively. I was attending museum and gallery exhibitions and soaking in every bit of information about a painting that I could gather in my mind.

How did this all begin? How did a thirty–six–year–old wife and mother of five children become so excited about painting?

Before I met Rosella, I took painting lessons for about three years with Dona. She is a local artist, and I enjoyed weekly classes at her home studio. I painted at my home every day of the week following each class. Whatever I learned in class, I duplicated and reinforced that lesson in other paintings at home. My kitchen table was my studio. After the children left for school, I covered our table with newspaper and got out my brushes, paints and canvas. Some days I was still painting when the children arrived home from school!

From the beginning, I learned to exhibit my artworks in shows in the tri–state area with my local artist friends. It felt very strange to me. I timidly presented my paintings at those first art shows. Dona taught me the basics of painting. She encouraged me to work from my imagination. She also introduced me to the need for entering my completed paintings in local and regional art shows. It was so intimidating to me, and it was exciting at the same time. During these first few years, I met and became friends with other local artists as we traveled together to enter our work in shows. We attended the opening receptions together. We helped each other as we took turns driving to the various locations for deliveries, picking up rejected works, attending receptions, and removing artworks at the end.

Eventually, I was ready to go in a new direction. I began taking every painting course offered by an instructor at the Hoyt Institute of Fine Arts in New Castle, Pennsylvania, from 1980 to 1985. I advanced to getting my paintings juried into major national exhibitions. I traveled to New York City to attend the opening reception at the Audubon National in 1984. This was my first time traveling alone on a plane to attend a national art exhibition where my painting was on display. It was a massive step for me to be at that show.

I took painting courses with David in the early 80s. He took my thoughts in new directions, and my interest in painting was solidified. I knew this was the life I was meant to live. I thrived, and I began showing my work in national exhibitions under his tutelage.

This trip to Mount Pocono with Rosella would be the first time I entered an academic program in art.

I was excited, and at the same time, I was anxious. I had no idea what to expect; nevertheless, I was taking a step in a new direction. This was the first time I was going to take a class that would be graded by a professor of art.

Rosella and I packed up my red sports car with our painting gear. We had a list of recommended items to bring with us. In addition, we had prepared our painting surfaces, as instructed. Once we arrived, we would be ready to begin painting outdoors in the Pocono Mountains for the 10–day landscape painting experience. On the afternoon before we were set to leave, a series of tornadoes ripped through Pennsylvania.

Rosella and I departed on the morning of June 1, 1985. This was the morning after the historical tornadoes. As we drove the I–80 corridor across the state, we saw one nightmare scene of destruction after another. Our minds were set on the trip ahead of us, and we drove through entire areas where everything in sight looked like it had been bombed. Buildings were smashed. Trees were broken off like toothpicks. Yet, we observed tiny wildflowers blooming along the hillsides. Occasionally, we stopped to get out of the car and take photos of the blooming flowers and the clear skies. A significant tornado did not deter us from leaving on our new adventure.

After crossing the state, we stopped to spend our first night in bed and breakfast. The following day we reached the location where we would participate in the workshop. We had no idea what the next ten days would be like, but we were excited to begin.

Our group of fifteen brave artists painted outdoors every day regardless of the weather. We had rainstorms and plunging temperatures. We were dropped off at a different location every morning. At lunchtime, we had a bag lunch that was prepared for us. We continued to paint until late afternoon. We returned to the van with our painting gear, wet paintings, and sketchbooks. Evenings were spent in a recreation hall where we tried to dry out our wet socks and shoes on the fireplace's hearth. We also worked on the paintings we had started on the location that day. This was a first–time experience for me to be painting by remembering what I had seen earlier in the day.

At night, we slept in outdoor structures with roll–down canvas sides. In the darkness, we chatted about the day's events in the Pocono Mountains and the latest headlines in the news. It was cold and damp. We snuggled deep into our sleeping bags to keep warm, one by one, the talking ceased, and we drifted off to sleep.

After we were back home, our grades arrived. Rosella received an A. I got a B+.

I've realized that the things that are not graded are often essential life lessons. We did not let a massive set of tornadoes change our plans. We traveled across our state to attend the workshop despite the destruction we watched along the way. The chilly, overcast mornings did not prevent us from going outside each day to paint with our new friends.

Our trip opened my mind to new priceless possibilities of entering an academic art program at Slippery Rock University of Pennsylvania. My pursuit of the BFA in Painting began in the fall semester of 1985. Two months after completing the outdoor landscape painting workshop, When I walked into my first university art classroom, I was almost forty–two years old.

With God, all things are possible.
Luke 1:37 English Standard Version.

Bonus

You can read the historical context of this story.

On May 31, 1985...a deadly tornado outbreak...ripped through the region, causing the second deadliest natural disaster in Pennsylvania's history. 43 separate tornadoes would claim 89 lives and upwards of 700 million dollars in damage. 65 fatalities in Pennsylvania place May 31, 1985, a tornado outbreak second only to the 1889 Johnstown Flood, which claimed 2,200 lives.

Jeff Sherry, Museum Educator, Hagen History Center
Tornado Outbreak in Pennsylvania, May 31, 1985.

©April 8, 2022. Lynda McKinney Lambert. All rights reserved.

Published on April 8, 2022
The Evergreen Journal, Walking by Inner Vision Blog.

Visibility

by Lynda McKinney Lambert

The scene is subdued.
Visibility is low.

I feel like I am standing in an art gallery, viewing a delicate landscape painting. The morning panorama was created by a highly skilled watercolor artist who carefully mixes the transparent colors of the pigments. I think about what I would choose to paint today if I was going to do a landscape painting.

Everything is so diffused by the atmosphere. I stand a moment and try to memorize this feeling of mystery that surrounds me.

This particular day looks fragile, yet it has a heft to it, like the heavy white handmade paper that absorbs the soft colors of the artist's brush strokes.

Before dawn, I slipped my bare feet into my purple boots and put on my soft grey jacket over my long floral nightgown. I walked onto the porch's wooden planks with my two dogs as we do every morning.

As we padded down onto the sidewalk, I could feel cool raindrops splashing gently onto us. It was thicker than the mist, but I knew instinctively it was the beginning of the predicted rainy day.

The early morning light is a soft grey wash. The invisible artist was at work just outside my office window. I see the stately Norway Maple tree that stands at attention like a watchman guarding the space between the meditation garden and the oversized black two–story garage that is shaped like a barn.

In the distance, the low lighting flattens the surface of the painting because I can barely see the trees in the woods. It's too early in the Spring season for leaves on the trees. Likewise, I cannot see the reflection of light on the water's surface flowing downstream on the Connoquenessing Creek beneath the ridge.

I listen for crows calling across the treetops, but all is quiet this morning. The only sound I can hear is the traffic splashing on the highway as they move East and West across the bridge just beyond the house.

I pause for a moment, pull my shoulders back, and am conscious of my inhalation. I breathe deeply as I inhale and hold it for a few seconds. My body connects to my mind, and my thoughts expand with every breath. I silently say, "thank you, God, for breath."

I can feel the misty air filling my lungs as my diaphragm expands. As I take another breath, I lift my hands upwards and move them slowly downwards as I exhale. Finally, I close my eyes and whisper, "This is a good day, Lord. I thank you now for this quiet time with You in the early morning."

Rainy spring days like this one seem fragile and sensitive. This will be a good day for doing something personal and private or going out with a friend to get a pedicure.

I know that it won't be long until the days are much brighter, and I will be going out to begin the spring clean–up in the yard and flower gardens. But, not today.

Published

Revised from the original story posted in
The Evergreen Journal #11, Walking by Inner Vision Blog.
March 25, 2022.

The Evergreen Journal #11 Visibility March 25, 2022 Lynda
McKinney Lambert American Author (lyndalambert.com).

About Lynda McKinney Lambert

Pennsylvania author/artist, Lynda McKinney Lambert writes award–winning books, thoughtful personal essays, and spare poems. Lynda explores life experiences through writing and art.

Lynda is a retired Professor of Fine Arts and Humanities, Geneva College, Beaver Falls, PA. With her extensive background in Fine Arts, English Literature, and Humanities, she creates mixed–media fiber art for exhibitions and her writings that are published internationally. Lynda's Judeo–Christian worldview reveals wonders.

She lives and works in rural western Pennsylvania in The Village of Wurtemburg. Lynda authored 4 books and her work appears in a number of prestigious anthologies in the United States, United Kingdom, and Hong Kong.

Website: http://www.lyndalambert.com

Publications

First Snow, by Lynda McKinney Lambert, Finishing Line Press, (2 January 2020).

Star Signs: New & Selected Poems, Lynda McKinney Lambert, author/publisher, (16 July 2019).

Star Signs: New & Selected Poems, Lynda McKinney Lambert, Audio by Lillian Yves and Vincent Lee Grayson, (21 October 2021).

Songs for the Pilgrimage, Lynda McKinney Lambert, author/publisher, (20 April 2021).
    Bard edition narrated by Polly Slavet at Perkins Library.

Walking by Inner Vision: Stories & Poems, by Lynda McKinney Lambert, author/publisher, (22 February 2017).
    Bard edition narrated by Polly Slavet at Perkins Library.

Walking by Inner Vision: Stories & Poems, Audio by Lillian Yves, (22 May 2019).

Concerti: Psalms for the Pilgrimage, published by Kota Press, 2002

Lynda McKinney Lambert

Flashes in the Sky (Ballad Nonfiction)

by Marlene Mesot

There is nothing wrong or right,
About the experience of that night.
it was just an observation of mine,
That could have been a situation so unkind,
Had it been the fantasy,
My mind made it out to be.

It was dark, outside lights on.
The ground was cool but the air was warm.
My 12 year old English Mastiff Toya on a leash,
And I with flashlight headed out. No small feat.
Both of us with eyesight poor,
Were out in the yard to explore.

We take her evening walks together.
Keeping her safe is so much better.
She has a habit of barking every time,
When she is let out on her own incline.
So we were out for her own sake,
To do her business post haste.

We walked down the driveway in our yard,
To near the gate where her way was barred.
The large yard is surrounded by a six foot high wire fence,
A safety precaution of worthwhile expense.
As she did her business there,
Of what I saw she was unaware.

Out of the corner of my eye,
A blink of light I thought I spied.
I turned my head left to look.
Again the sight in I took.
In the quiet of the night.
There was no other soul in sight.

The air was still. There was no breeze.
Above the skyline of the trees,
I saw rapid flashes of white light.
There was no sound to split the night.
It paused and then resumed again.
What was this strange happenin'?

I drew in breath with shock and awe,
My mouth agape as I took pause.
With little sleep your mind plays tricks.
Surely this couldn't be approaching alien spaceships!
It came in frequent, rapid bursts.
There was no sound. What on earth?

The white light was solid in its shape,
Not jagged arc lines as electricity might make.
It's rapid blinks came and went in uniform snatches,
Not intermittent like dots and dashes.
This blinking was silent, steady and fast.
We didn't wait to see how long it would last.

Could it be some silent thing,
Coming to unearth my being?
Of course not rational me said,
But I just wanted back to my bed.
Hurrying my dog Toya along,
We walked back, my footsteps strong.

Inside the house I went to get my son.
"Something strange outside. You have to see this one!'
To my son I did implore.
Calmly he walk toward the door.
He opened the inside door to our front porch.
Through the outside glass door he looked without a torch.

He too observed the silent, rapid bursts.
Then he told me without a curse,
"It's just heat lightning." he said with calm.
"But there's no rain, no thunder storm."
"Sometimes it happens just that way."
So I remember that experience until this day.

Heat lightning is nothing new.
But when your mind has gone askew,
You conjure scenarios from air thin,
Giving the ordinary a different spin.
Keep in mind who has your care,
From beginning to end, everywhere.

Was God saying, in His way,
I watch over you, night or day?
Was He saying all along,
You are weak, but I am strong?
Was He saying without fail,
I have a plan that will prevail?

Marlene and Tracker, 1/24/2011

Split Screen Weather

by Marlene Mesot

Rainbow, 4/23/2007

Double Rainbow, 4/23/2007

It was not uncommon to run into unusual weather patterns commuting to work, as my husband Albert and I lived in Virginia and worked in Greensboro NC for 15 years before he retired. I retired later, six months after he passed away. The drive took around an hour each way depending on traffic and road conditions, such as road construction. We have encountered accidents but fortunately never had been in one.

On one particular stormy morning commute on April 23, 2007, we experienced sighting two different rainbows during that storm. I've heard of seeing rainbows following a storm, but not during. I actually have pictures of them both. At one point following these incidents during the trip, Al pulled into a gas station for a few minutes. The rain was so severe that visibility was difficult. Fog complicated the situation and Al said that he couldn't see more than a foot in front of him. It looked as if someone was literally dumping buckets of water down from the sky in sheets of liquid. He called work on his cell phone to explain why we might be a few minutes late. Fortunately our supervisor was understanding and said no problem and to take our time. It was a relief to arrive without mishap.

The sky was a dark gray wall all around looking like twilight instead of early morning. It was very windy and the rain could be heard pelting the roof of the car. Street lights were on as we passed towns along the long stretch of highway, but it was dark except for the other car lights where fields and woods lined the road.

We were both sitting in front and my husband told me where to look when he saw a rainbow appear. I quickly got out my cell phone, a flip phone at the time, but no internet, just calls and picture taking capability. I tried to get the picture while the windshield wipers were in the down position and saved it. Not long after that he said there was a double rainbow and told me where to look. Still having my camera in hand, I again clicked and saved the picture.

The next weather story is even stranger.

The first time I experienced the following phenomenon was at my grandparents' camp. I was privileged to be able to go to my grandparents' camp frequently when I was growing up. Actually it was my Uncle Joe's property but my grandparents made it the home away from home that it was. In 1954, when I was three, Uncle Joe purchased a lot and a half on Deering Lake in Deering, New Hampshire and built the camp with the help of my grandfather Joe and Uncle's friends.

I remember one particular day the grownups were playing horse shoes in the open lot beside the camp. At some point that afternoon, I was standing there in the sunshine when the women sitting at the picnic table shouted to look at the lake. Sure enough, the sky over the lake was clouded and dark. The water was rippling with lines as it moved and rain was pouring down. Yet, where I was standing the sun was out and the air was still. It appeared as if night was falling on the lake, but it was still daytime where we were.

Everyone hurried into their camps. We knew the storm would soon engulf us too.

Now back to the story of our commute from work. This time we were just turning onto the connecting road to the highway coming home from work on May 6, 2011. I was sitting in the back seat as we had a fellow co–worker who rode with us for six years in front. My husband Albert was driving. It was sunny with open land on my side of the car, the right side. Again my husband remarked about the storm he could see up ahead of us. We were going to be passing trees in a wooded area next and here is where the dividing line occurred. Again the sky was covered in a wall of dark gray clouds looking like nighttime. We could see the wind bending the trees and the rain pouring down. As we drove I watched the sunny area stop and the dark forbidding approach. Out of the passenger side window I snapped the picture. About half of the screen on the right has some of the hill with blue sky and sun shining on the grass, while the left side shows the tops of darkly bent trees and very dark sky above. It is as if someone created a split screen weather image from a computer program. But this was no computer generated image. It came from a flip cell phone and I saved the shot.

This picture is the header of my website, http://www.marlsmenagerie.com as well as a book cover. I am a Christian mystery writer so I think the dark and light actually from a real life situation make an intriguing statement for visitors.

73

Storms, 5/6/2011

About Marlene Mesot

Marlene Mesot, an only child, grandchild and niece from Manchester New Hampshire, and deceased husband Albert, have two sons, two grandchildren and English Mastiff dogs. She is legally blind and moderately deaf due to nerve damage at premature birth. She has loved writing since early childhood.

Marlene holds a Bachelor of Education degree from Keene State in Keene, New Hampshire and a Master's in Library and Information Studies from U–NC Greensboro, North Carolina.

Website: www.marlsmenagerie.com

Publications

4 Elements of Mystery Series

1 *The Purging Fire*, second edition, Marlene Mesot, Christian Faith Publishing, Meadville PA, (20 April 2018).

The Purging Fire, Marlene Mesot, Audio by Timothy G. Little, (25 September 2020).

2 *The Snowball Effect*, Marlene Mesot, author/publisher, (13 June 2021).

The Snowball Effect, Marlene Mesot, Audio by Timothy G. Little and Deb Wittner, (22 November 2021).

The Cat Stalker's Sonnets, Marlene Mesot, author/publisher, (16 March 2020).

Edgy Poetry, Marlene Mesot, author/publisher, (31 January 2021).

Deadly Poetry, Marlene Mesot, author/publisher, (2023).

The Author's Edge, Marlene Mesot, author/publisher, Foreword by Lynda McKinney Lambert, (12 April 2022).
> *The Author's Edge*, Audio by Timothy G. Little (28 June 2022).

The Spirit of One, Marlene Mesot, author/publisher, Audio by Timothy G. Little, (17 August 2022).

The Passion of Life's Storms

by Patty L. Fletcher

Rain swirls round with fury.
I can relate to its frustration.
Though I know my own words manifested my situation, I'm still
    not where I want or need to be.
I'm in a trap of my own making.
Every refuge has its price.

How do I rise to the next level of my life?
Where am I to go from here?

I know this is not the last step upon the path.
I feel lost.
Trees of darkness shadow.
Sun of purest white tries to break through.

I am what I am, yet I am more.
I thrust my fists outward,
Upward,
Downward,
Forward.

I continue placing one foot in front of the other.
I know to do otherwise brings no result.

I dream of more.
I desire a place in the world.

I continue placing one finger at a time on the keys.
My words come slowly.

I am shrouded in fog.
My life is bogged down in the swamp of doubt.
My spirit is sucked down in the quicksand of self–loathing.

I continue placing one foot in front of the other on the pathway.
My shroud falls away.
The sun shines with brilliance,
clear and bright just a little way in front of me.
I continue placing one foot in front of the other upon the
    pathway.

Birds sing notes of silver and gold.
Dogs bark sharp red bursts of staccato,
Voicing their displeasure at having their slumber in dark green
    shade disrupted as I pass.

I continue placing one foot in front of the other upon the
    pathway.
Again, I'm shrouded in gray mist.
Black clouds of misery boil in a purple sky above.
Red, blue, and yellow flashes of lightening crisscross the
    thunderous sky.

Thor roars his displeasure in black crashes of thunder,
Crushing my doubt and ignorance underneath the wheels of his
    chariot of fire.

The ground shifts beneath me.

I continue placing one foot in front of the other on the pathway.
The pathway is life.
Life must be lived.
Life is ever changing.

Again, my shroud falls away.
For every step I go forward I take more back.
I feel the ice–cold blue wind of sorrow.

I continue placing one foot in front of the other upon the
    pathway.
For to stop is to die.

Author Comments

In the early morning of Beltane, I authored this poem while walking in the first thunderstorm of the season with my guide Chief Seeing Eye® Dog Blue by my side.

As we walked, tears of rage, frustration, sadness, and deep longing for more rolled down my cheeks.

Though I knew I was in a good place, I also knew I wasn't where I would make my true mark on the world.

When we stopped so Blue could sniff out the best spot for his business a large crash of thunder split the silence the wind swirled as if catching the full brunt of my emotions and flung torrents of rain down upon me and how I did laugh.

Kneeling, I picked up Blue's leavings then, raising my face to the cleansing rain Mother Father God provided I began to know how to go forward in the passion of life's storms. The sun burst through the darkness with life giving warmth and golden joy and I began to know how to go forward in the passion of life's storms.

About Patty L. Fletcher

Patty L. Fletcher lives in Kingsport Tennessee where she works full time as a writer with the goal of bridging the great chasm which separates the disAbled from the non–disAbled. She is also a Social Media Marketing Assistant, public speaker and host of the Tell–It–to–the–World Marketing Podcast.

Website: https://pattysworlds.com/

Publications

Campbell's Rambles: How a Seeing Eye Dog Retrieved My Life, Patty L. Fletcher, author/publisher, (1 August 2014).

Tales from King Campbell Series
1 *Bubba Tails from the Puppy Nursery at Seeing Eye*, Claire Plaisted of Plaisted Publishing House, publisher, (3 October 2017).

Pathway to Freedom Broken & Healed Series
1 *How a Seeing Eye Dog Retrieved My Life*, Claire Plaisted of Plaisted Publishing House, publisher, (26 November 2020).

Patty and Blue in Kingsport, Tennessee, 6/10/2022

Dodging Tornados
in Tornado Alley

by Robert D. Sollars

I grew up in the Midwest, St. Joseph, MO, to be exact, and lived in North Dakota and Texas as well, in my first 42 years of life. Both in Missouri and Texas, it was called "Tornado Alley", for a very good reason. Ninety per cent of all tornados are seen in this rectangular area that reaches from Texas up through and into Minnesota and Wisconsin. It definitely encompassed my area of Missouri.

Personally, I've never been afraid of bad weather or tornados, even as a small kid, I just shrugged them off and wanted to watch them...but you do know how grandparents are about those sorts of things.

The only bad weather I didn't like, but muddled through, in my working life, were ice storms and snow, but that's another story. I've really liked tornados and never was scared or traumatized by them, actually enjoying watching and tracking them...I've been through, or seen, 10 of them since the late 60s.

In 1989, I was married with a 6-year-old son, living in a dilapidated 25-year-old trailer, on top of a hill, surrounded by farm fields and the gravel roads. I had one pass over the top of my trailer, at that point late at night, around 0200 hours, and all of a sudden, I heard a locomotive bearing down on us, seemingly a hundred miles an hour and getting so loud, threatening to run us over, with no tracks.

My first thought as I came to full consciousness was that it was awfully close and loud, because the railroad tracks are four or five miles away! As I looked around at the bedroom the walls of that old rat trap trailer were bowing in and out by a good six to ten inches and the windows were flapping in the wind. Within 10 seconds it was all over and we went back to sleep, after a few minutes to calm down.

When I awoke the next morning...I found out that we had a new temporary security account at work with an automotive parts warehouse that had sustained damage. It had one side and the roof blown off, slicing through trees at an upwards slant through 50–foot–tall oak.

But the real story occurred on May 10, 2003. My new wife and I were still living in the same location, albeit with a newer trailer. She wasn't working that day, but I was, in Kansas City, MO. We were having ever increasing thunderstorms and the possibility of tornados throughout the afternoon and evening, the weather alerts had been being given for the past five hours or so, for 0900 hours.

To me it was no big deal...I knew what to do and helped a couple of my security officers and posts get their emergency plans together during my shift as A.M. Operations Supervisor.

My wife called and said she was scared to death, while hiding in the closet with a futon pad and her cat Creamsicle who was an orange and white male. There were no tornados at home, but I decided to take off work and go home to comfort and be with her. She had never lived in this area before and didn't know or like these Tasmanian Devils.

I started home from the office at around 1:00 P.M. As I got on the I–635 north, a tornado was seen passing through Kansas City, KS. about two miles from where I was. It passed over the highway about three minutes after I passed by that location.

Ten minutes later I was transitioning off of I–635 onto northbound I–29, after hearing a report of a tornado tearing up houses, landscaping, storage bins, etc. that had occurred about two minutes in front of me. I passed by the site and seen the devastation that it had wrought. Houses blown apart, cars, pieces of houses under construction, and construction materials were scattered literally everywhere, including a heavy piece of machinery tumbled on its side, just off the highway to the east of I–29.

Five to seven minutes up the road, getting ready to pass Kansas City International airport, another report stated that a tornado had been spotted just off the airport and passed over the highway two minutes in front of me, but no damage was reported, although it did touch down on one of the runways...again just off the highway.

I went along my merry way, watching for any signs of tornados or heavy rain on the way north to home. Yet again...less than five minutes later, another tornado passed behind me, close to the airport again, going the opposite direction (west).

As strange as it sounds, but it's what happens during an outbreak of these things, 10 minutes later, another one was seen in a farm field on the west side of the highway, and had passed three minutes before I got there, fortunately no damage. Lastly, my wife called me and said that one had been spotted just south of St. Joseph and for me to be careful. I was, because it had already passed in front of me by two minutes!

My wife—still holding her cat Cream, who was extremely

indignant about being held so tight for so long—gave me a hug, kisses, and started crying. I calmed her down and we spent a wonderful evening together while cuddling.

My wife keeps telling me, during tornados, that they will eventually find me in Arizona and sure enough they are searching for me! Twice in 2020, tornados were spotted in suburban areas of the North Phoenix area. Fortunately, they were 25 or so miles away and didn't get close, but other tornados have been further away down here. I keep telling her "They're getting closer and closer!" then laugh as she utters a string of expletives and whacks me on the arm.

Again, to me anyway, tornados are a part of living in the Midwest and not a big deal. I've never been through an earthquake, hurricane, or such, but...always hoping for the experience.

About Robert D. Sollars

Robert D. Sollars has more than three decades of experience in the security field. He has held various management positions at both national and regional security companies in St. Joseph and Kansas City, Missouri.

Robert has three children and has always been concerned with their safety at school. Robert and his wife, Eileen, now live in Phoenix, Arizona with a very dutiful guardian watch cat, Brigadier General Jasmine Squeakers Long Hair, Chief of Cat Fleet Operations and Security.

After going blind in July 2003, just six weeks after moving to the Phoenix area, Robert continued in his quest to increase security awareness. Since that time, he has started a blog that is published twice weekly on his website, www.robertdsollars.com, He has also published nonfiction books and numerous other articles and appeared on many local and national TV and radio shows as an expert.

Website: http://www.robertdsollars.com

Publications

Nonfiction

Murder at Work: A practical Guide for Prevention, Robert D. Sollars, DLD Books, ed. (5 May 2020).

One is too Many: Recognizing and Preventing Workplace violence, Robert D. Sollars, Demon & Hunter Publishing, (24 January 2018).

Unconventional Customer Service: How to Break the Rules and Provide Unparalleled Customer Service, Robert D. Sollars, DLD Books, ed. (23 October 2018).

Murder in the Classroom: A Practical Guide for Prevention, Robert D. Sollars, DLD Books, ed. (10 June 2018).

Never to Grow Up: Preventing Violence in Our Schools, Robert D. Sollars, Demon & Hunter Publishing, (31 October 2009).

Adult Fiction

Between Two and Other Tales of Love and Romance by Robert D. Sollars, author/publisher, (6 November 2022).

Evil Does as Evil Is: and Other Dark Tales, Robert D. Sollars, author/publisher, (5 December 2021).

Legend of Three Series
1 *The Rise of Marpatronia* (15 August 2021).